Contents

Some words are shown in bold, **like this.** You can find out what they mean by looking in the glossary.

Meet the mammals

Dogs, squirrels, sheep and elephants are all mammals. Mammals are animals that have hair on their bodies and that feed their babies with milk from the mother.

Dogs and humans have lots of hair, so they are **classified** as mammals.

Animal Classifications

Mammals

Angela Royston

Raintree is an imprint of Capstone Global Library Limited, a company incorporated in England and Wales having its registered office at 7 Pilgrim Street, London, EC4V 6LB – Registered company number: 6695582

www.raintreepublishers.co.uk
myorders@raintreepublishers.co.uk

Edited by Helen Cox Cannons, Clare Lewis and
        Abby Colich
Designed by Steve Mead
Picture research by Tracy Cummins
Production by Victoria Fitzgerald
Originated by Capstone Global Library Ltd
Printed and bound in China

ISBN 978 1 406 28740 0 (hardback)
18 17 16 15 14
10 9 8 7 6 5 4 3 2 1

ISBN 978 1 406 28747 9 (paperback)
19 18 17
10 9 8 7 6 5 4 3 2

British Library Cataloguing in Publication Data
A full catalogue record for this book is available from the British Library.

Acknowledgements
We would like to thank the following for permission to reproduce photographs: Capstone Press: Karon Dubke, 27; Getty Images: Dr Clive Bromhall, 25, Mark Carwardine, 13, 29 Top; Shutterstock: Anan Kaewkhammul, Design Element, Bailey0ne, 4, CanuckStock, 19, Christopher Elwell, 23, Four Oaks, 15, glenda, 18, Ivan Kuzmin, 7, Jarry, 20, 29 Bottom, Ken Wolter, 12, Kirsanov Valeriy Vladimirovich, 21, lightpoet, 11, Cover, Monkey Business Images, 26, Oleg Znamenskiy, 6, Seleznev Oleg, 8, 29 Middle, Stuart G Porter, 10, T.W. van Urk, 5, worldswildlifewonders, 17; SuperStock: Minden Pictures, 14; Thinkstock: Alan Jeffery, 24, Andre Anita, 9, Jiri Haureljuk, 16, 28, Photoservice, 22.
We would like to thank Michael Bright for his invaluable help in the preparation of this book.

Every effort has been made to contact copyright holders of material reproduced in this book. Any omissions will be rectified in subsequent printings if notice is given to the publisher.

All the Internet addresses (URLs) given in this book were valid at the time of going to press. However, due to the dynamic nature of the Internet, some addresses may have changed, or sites may have changed or ceased to exist since publication. While the author and publisher regret any inconvenience this may cause readers, no responsibility for any such changes can be accepted by either the author or the publisher.

Two lambs feed on milk, which they suck from the mother sheep.

Scientists sort living things into groups. This is called **classification.** Each group of living things is different from other groups in particular ways.

Body shape

Mammals are part of a bigger group called **vertebrates**. This group also includes **reptiles** and birds. All vertebrates have a backbone and a hard **skeleton** inside their bodies. The skeleton gives their body its shape.

Giraffes have the longest legs and longest neck of any mammal.

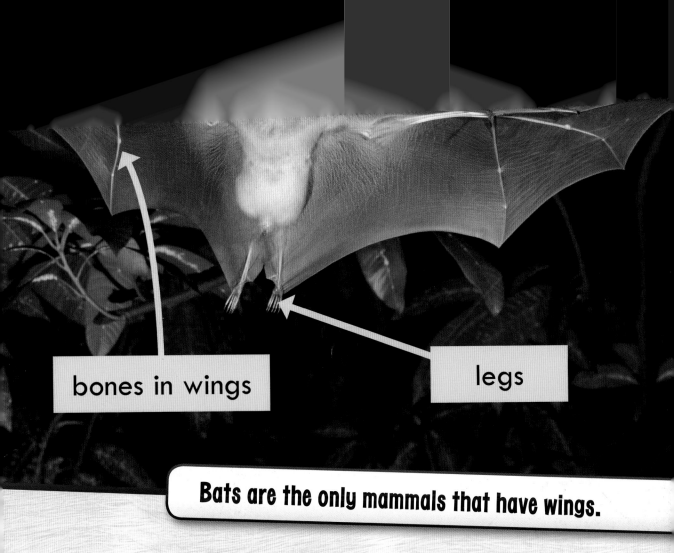

bones in wings

legs

Bats are the only mammals that have wings.

Most mammals have four legs, or two legs and two arms. Bats are mammals, but they have two legs and two wings. The wings are made of long, thin finger bones, with skin stretched between them.

Hair and fur

A mammal has hair that grows from its skin. Hair protects the skin and helps to keep the mammal warm. Some mammals, such as wolves, have thick hair. Others, such as elephants, have only a few hairs.

A camel's hair protects its skin from the hot sun.

A polar bear lives in the icy Arctic.
Its thick hair helps to keep it warm.

Mammals are **warm blooded**, which means
that they make heat using the energy from
food. Blood carries the heat all around
their bodies.

Cats

Mammals are **classified** into smaller groups and **families.** The cat family includes big cats, such as lions, cheetahs and tigers, as well as smaller pet cats. All cats look similar. For example, they have long backs and most have long tails.

A cheetah bends its long back as it runs.

It is easy to see that a lynx is a type of cat.

Cats have sharp claws and sharp teeth. They need them because they are **carnivores**. Carnivores eat meat from other animals.

Sea mammals

Sea mammals, including seals, dolphins and whales, live in the sea. Seals have thick fur, but most sea mammals, such as walruses and whales, have almost no hair.

Seals spend some time on land but they hunt for food in the sea.

The blue whale is the largest animal that has ever lived.

Instead of legs and arms, sea mammals have **flippers**, which they use to swim. Unlike fish, sea mammals cannot breathe in water. They have to come to the surface to breathe.

Giving birth

Instead of laying eggs, almost all mammals give birth to babies. The babies are small, but have the same body shape as their parents. Some mammals have several babies at a time. Others have one or two.

This dog has six puppies, which all look like her.

An elephant usually has one baby calf at a time.

All mammal mothers make milk in special parts of their body called **mammary glands**. Babies feed on their mother's milk until they are old enough to eat other food.

Marsupials

Kangaroos and koalas are both **marsupials**. Female marsupials have a special **pouch**. A baby marsupial is born when it is still tiny and not fully formed. It crawls into its mother's pouch, where it feeds on milk and grows bigger.

A kangaroo baby is safe in its mother's pouch.

Young koalas stay close to their mothers even after they have left the pouch.

A baby marsupial is called a joey. When the joey is big enough, it leaves the pouch and explores the world.

Looking after young

Mammals take care of their young until they are old enough to look after themselves. Baby mammals stay close to their mothers, who try to keep them safe from **predators**.

Newborn deer can stand and walk when they are only a few hours old.

A tiger cub practises stalking. It moves forward slowly then pounces.

Baby mammals learn many skills from their mothers. For example, tiger cubs learn how to hunt for food.

Rodents

Mice, hamsters, squirrels and prairie dogs all belong to a group of mammals called **rodents.** Many female rodents have lots of babies at the same time. A group of babies is called a **litter.**

All rodents have four large front teeth and gnaw their food.

A house mouse can have many litters of babies every year.

Baby rodents grow up fast! A house mouse starts to have her own babies when she is just two months old. She may produce 150 babies a year!

Herds and packs

Mammals that feed on plants, such as zebra and buffalo, live in large groups called **herds**. Living in a group makes it easier for these animals to stay safe from **predators**. Some mammal predators hunt together in groups called packs.

These zebras watch out for danger as they graze on the grass.

Prairie dogs leave their underground homes to feed.

Smaller mammals, such as **rodents** and rabbits, **burrow** under the ground. For example, prairie dogs live together in vast underground "towns".

Monkeys and apes

Monkeys, lemurs and apes belong to a group of mammals called **primates**. Monkeys mostly live high among the trees. They leap from branch to branch and tree to tree.

Some monkeys use their tail like an extra arm or leg to grip onto a branch.

A chimpanzee uses a rock as a tool to crack open nuts.

Apes include humans, so other apes are more like us than other animals. Apes have no tail and can stand on their two back legs.

One amazing mammal!

Humans are perhaps the most amazing mammal. Humans can speak, read and write. They can compose music and invent complicated machines. They can discuss ideas and plan for the future.

Human children take many years to grow up because they have so much to learn!

Humans love and care for other animals. This girl looks after her pet cat.

Humans understand the world better than any other animal. Can we use that understanding to make the world a better place for all animals to live in?

Quiz

Look at the pictures below and read the clues. Can you remember the names of these mammals? Look back in the book if you need help.

1. I am safe inside my mother's **pouch.** What am I?

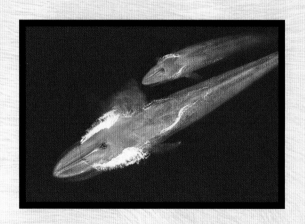

2. I live in the sea but I breathe in air. What am I?

3. I live in the desert. My hair protects me from the sun. What am I?

4. I am a **rodent** I have four large front teeth. What am I?

Glossary

burrow animal's underground home; digging an underground home

carnivore animal that eats other animals for food

classification system that scientists use to divide living things into separate groups

classified put into a group according to special things shared by that group

flipper hard, flat part of a sea mammal's body, which it uses to swim

herd large group of animals

litter number of babies born at the same time

mammary gland part of a female mammal's body that can make milk

marsupial mammal that gives birth to young that are not fully formed and continue to grow in the mother's pouch

pouch pocket-like body part on the outside of the body

predator animal that kills other animals for food

primate member of a group of mammals that have hands and hand-like feet. Monkeys, apes and humans are primates.

reptile member of a group of animals that have a dry, scaly skin

rodent member of a group of mammals that have four large front teeth, which they use to gnaw food

vertebrate animal that has a backbone and skeleton inside its body

warm blooded able to make body heat from food

Find out more

Books

Mammals (Deadly Factbook), Steve Backshall (Orion Books, 2012)

Mammals (True or False), Melvin and Gilda Berger (Scholastic, 2011)

RSPB First Book of Mammals, Anita Ganeri and David Chandler (A & C Black, 2011)

Whales and Dolphins (Mad About), Anita Ganeri (Ladybird, 2009)

Why do Mammals Have Fur?, Pat Jacobs (Franklin Watts, 2014)

Websites

kids.sandiegozoo.org/animals/mammals

The kids' section of the San Diego Zoo website includes photos and information about mammals. Click the small photos to find out about particular animals. Don't miss the games, videos and animal cams at the top.

www.nhm.ac.uk/kids-only

The "kids only" section of the Natural History Museum website includes the blue whale and the giant sloth, two of the stars of the museum.

Index